REPUTABLE DESIGN

this book belongs to

____

____

____

COLOR TEST PAGE

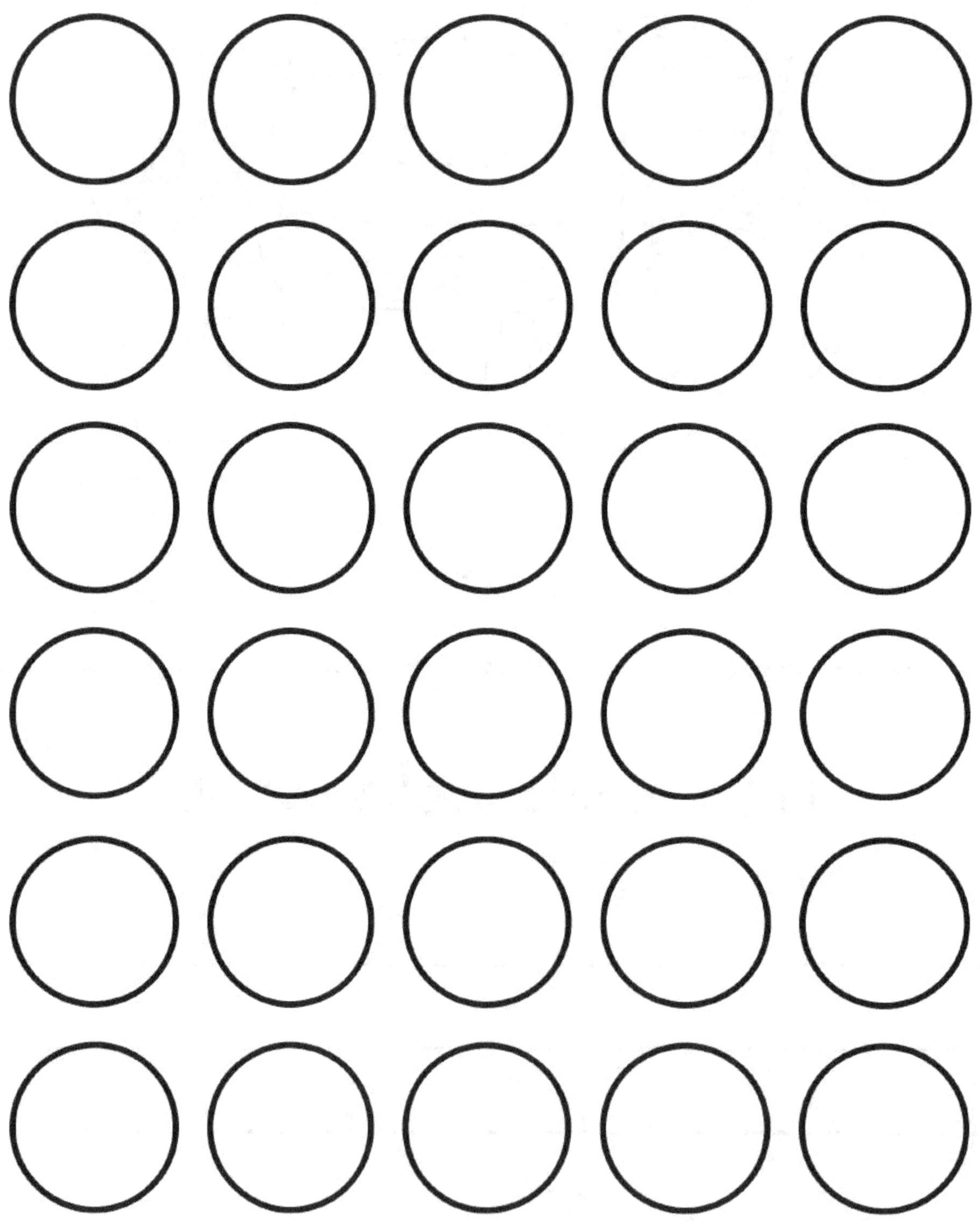

COLOR TEST PAGE

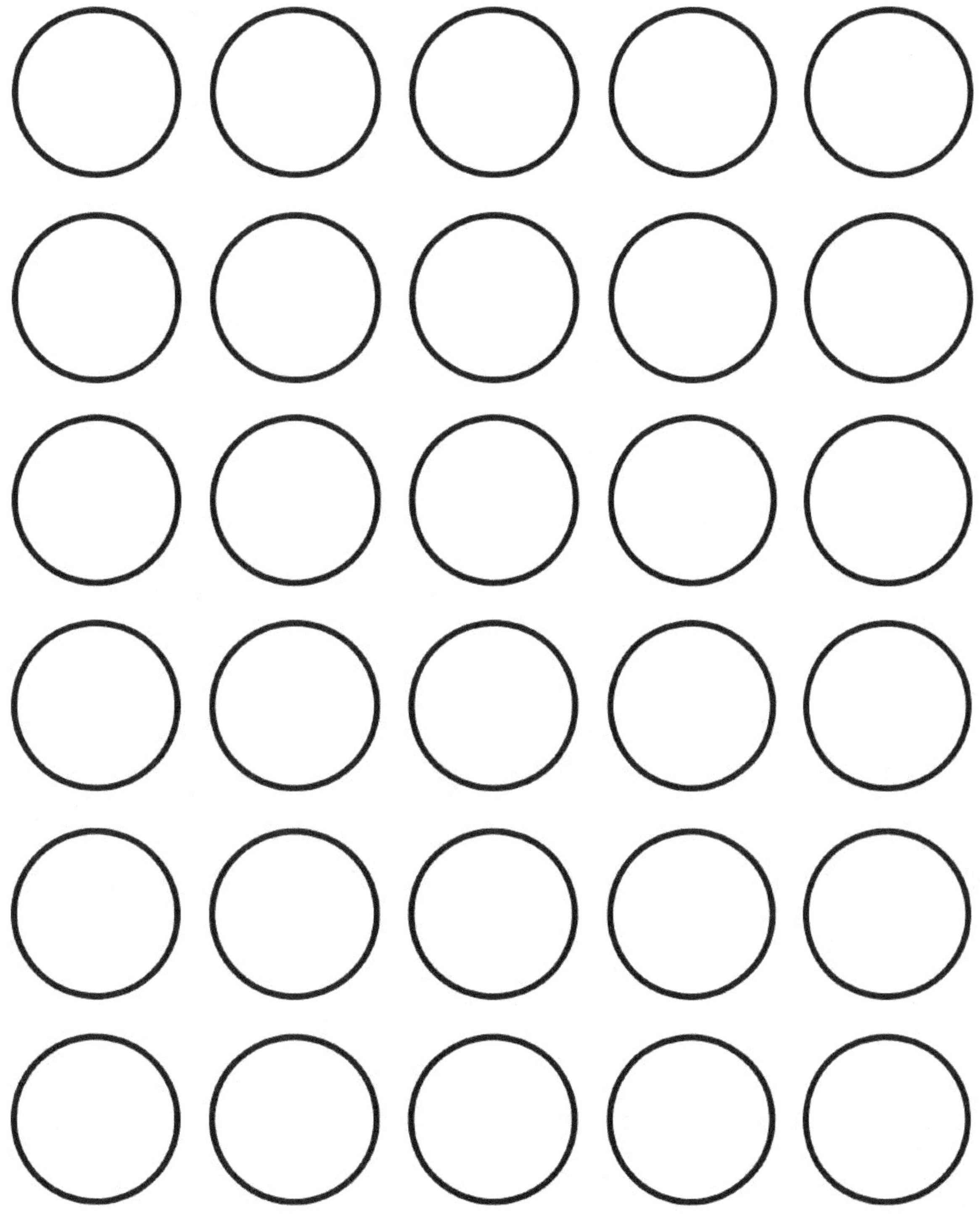

COLOR TEST PAGE

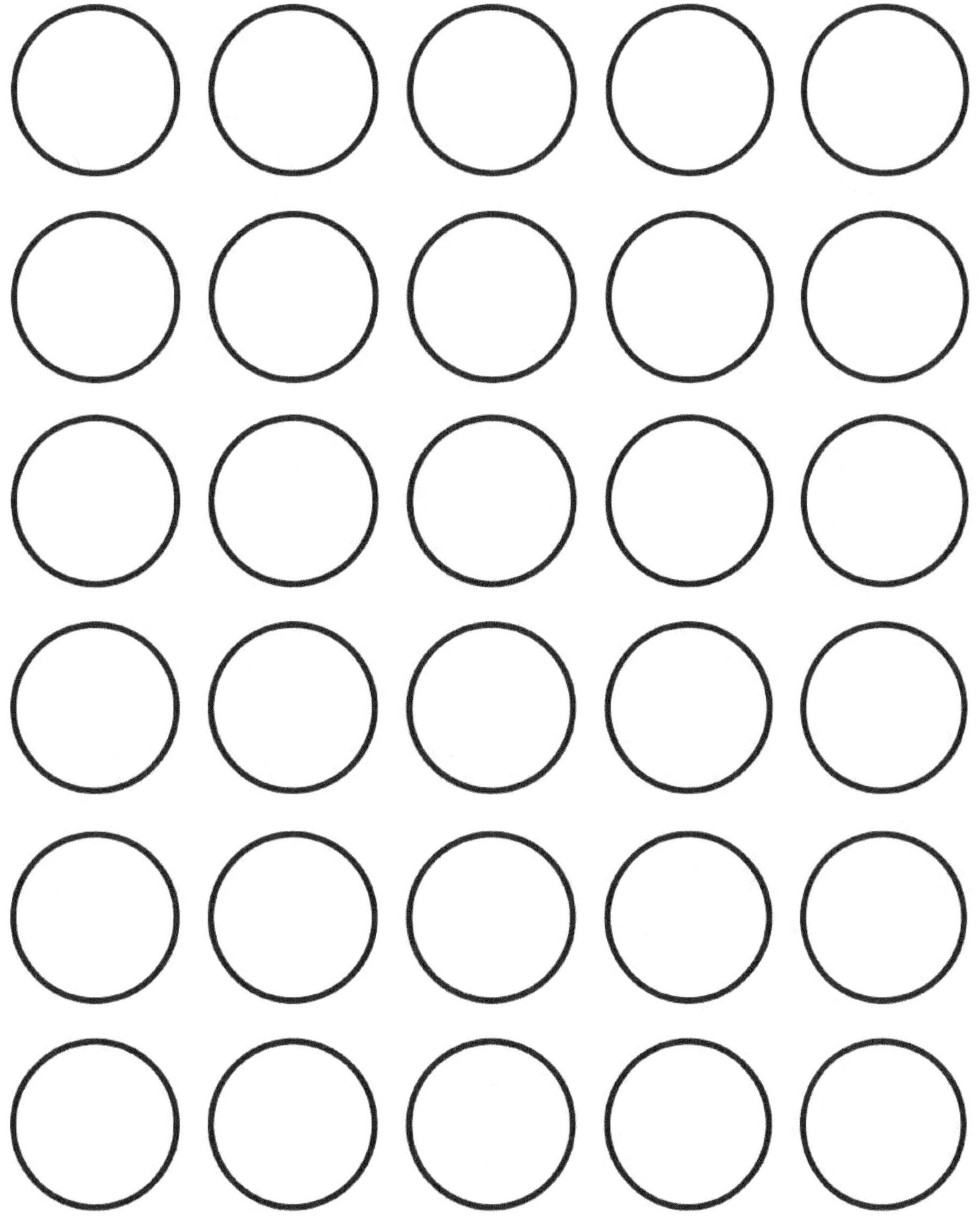

Love Muffins

FRIENDS
FOREVER!

COLOR TEST PAGE

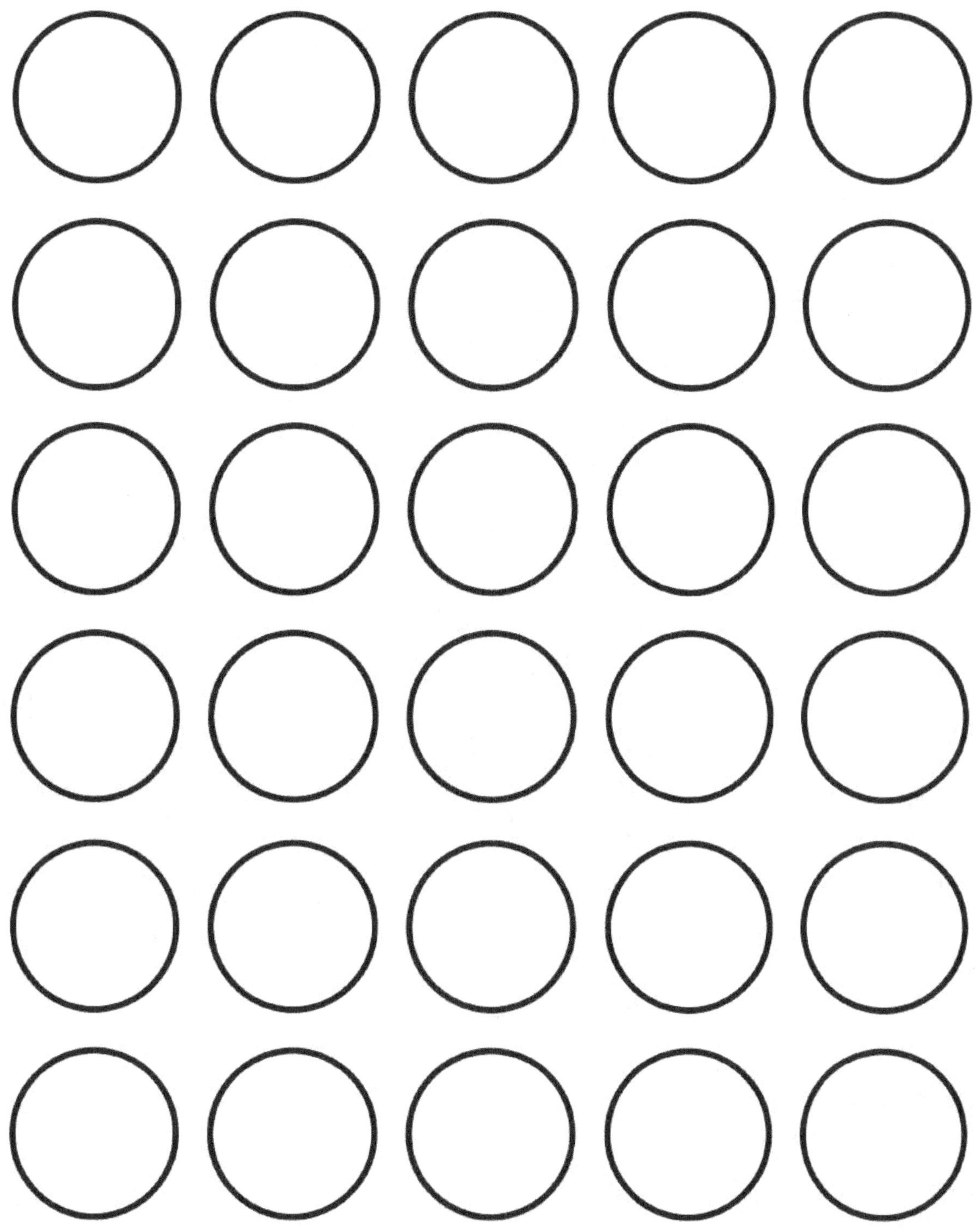

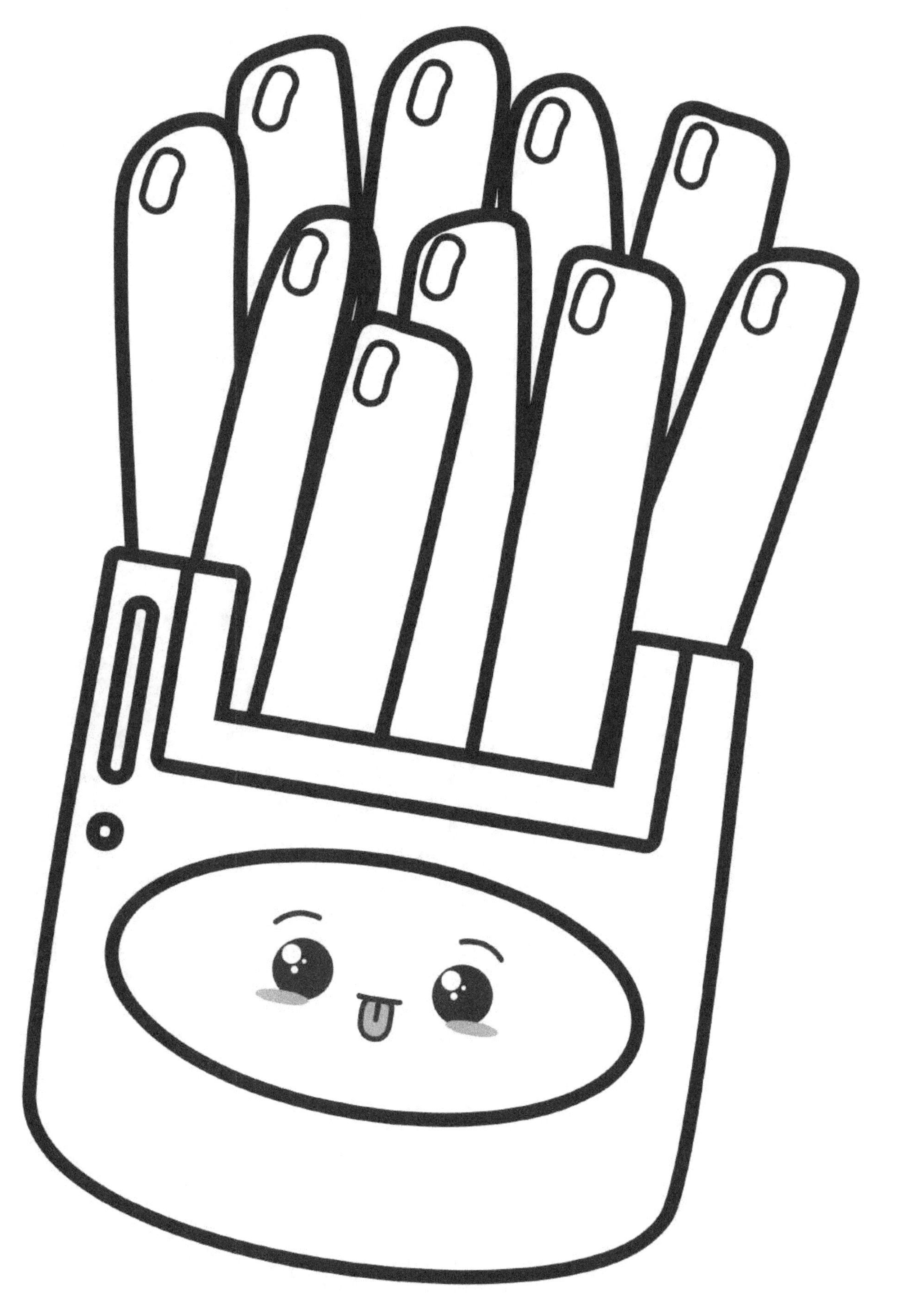

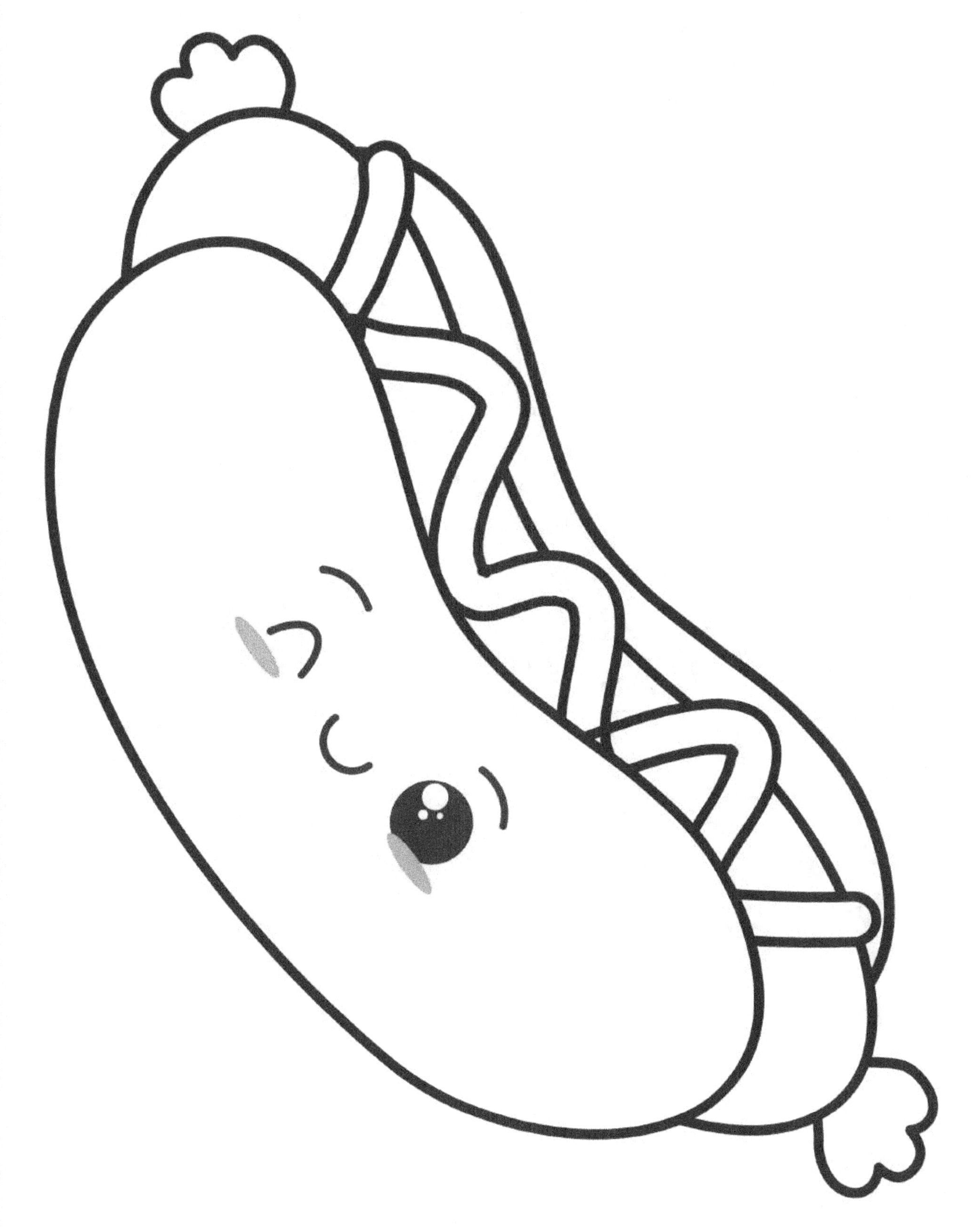

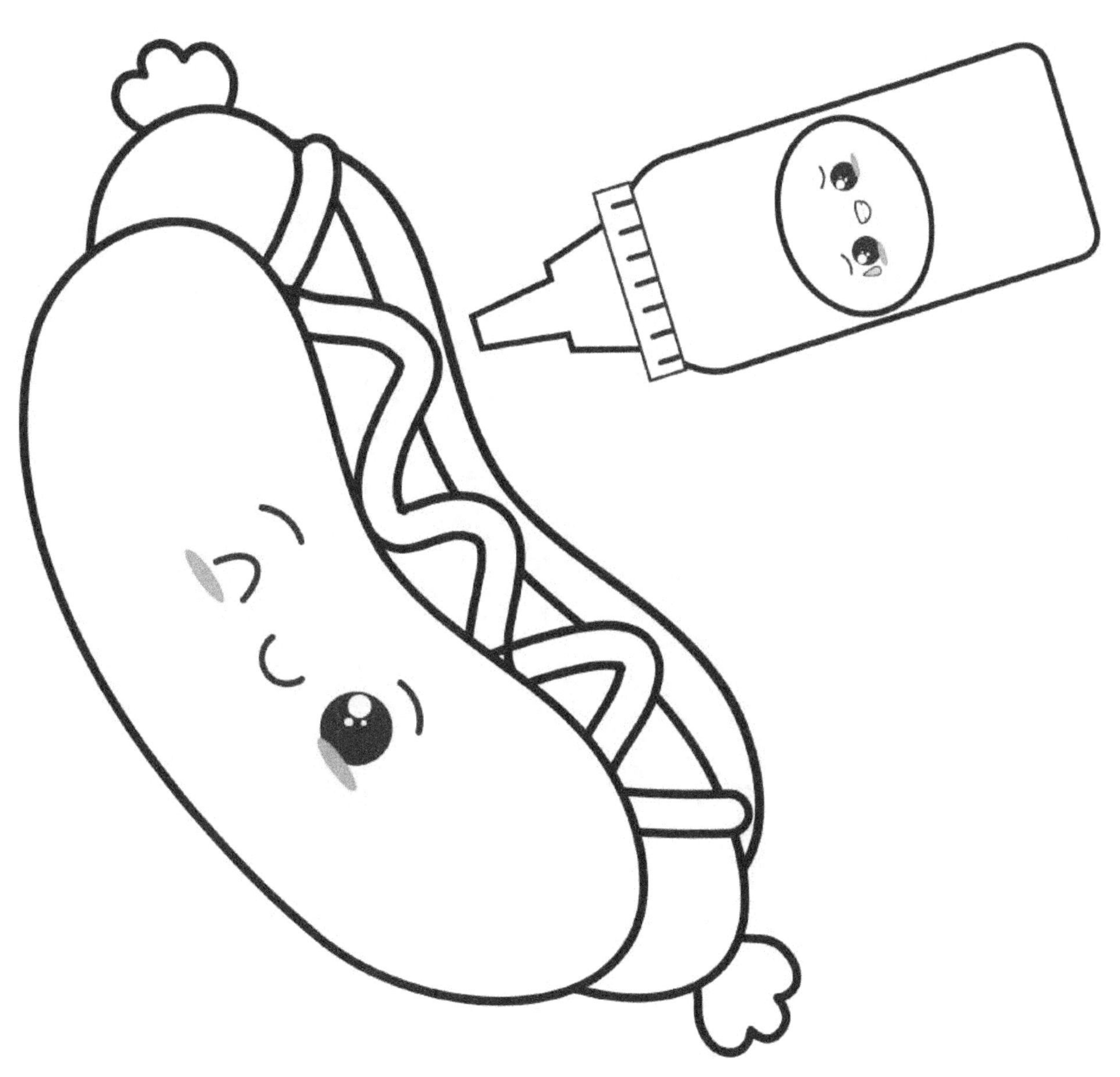

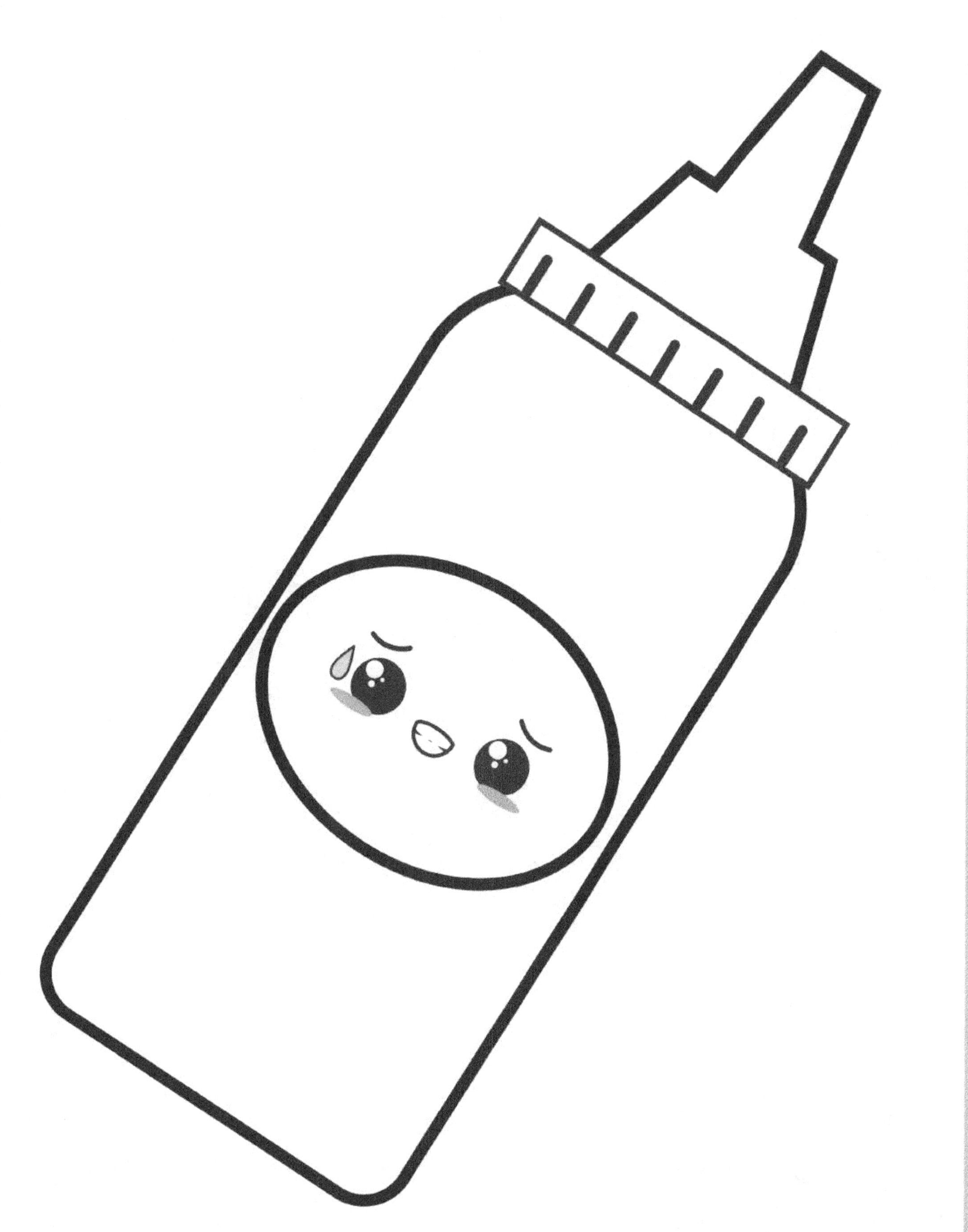

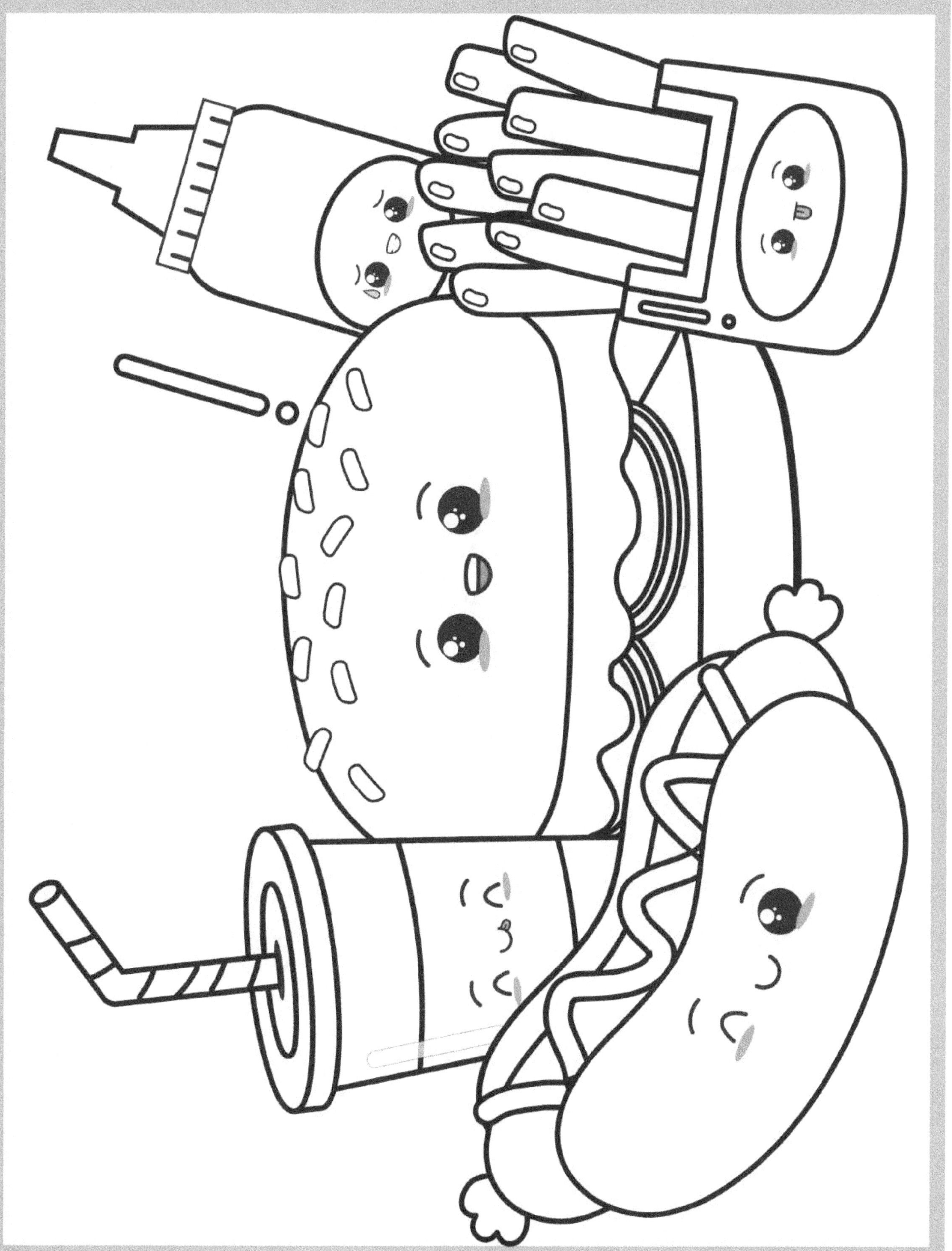

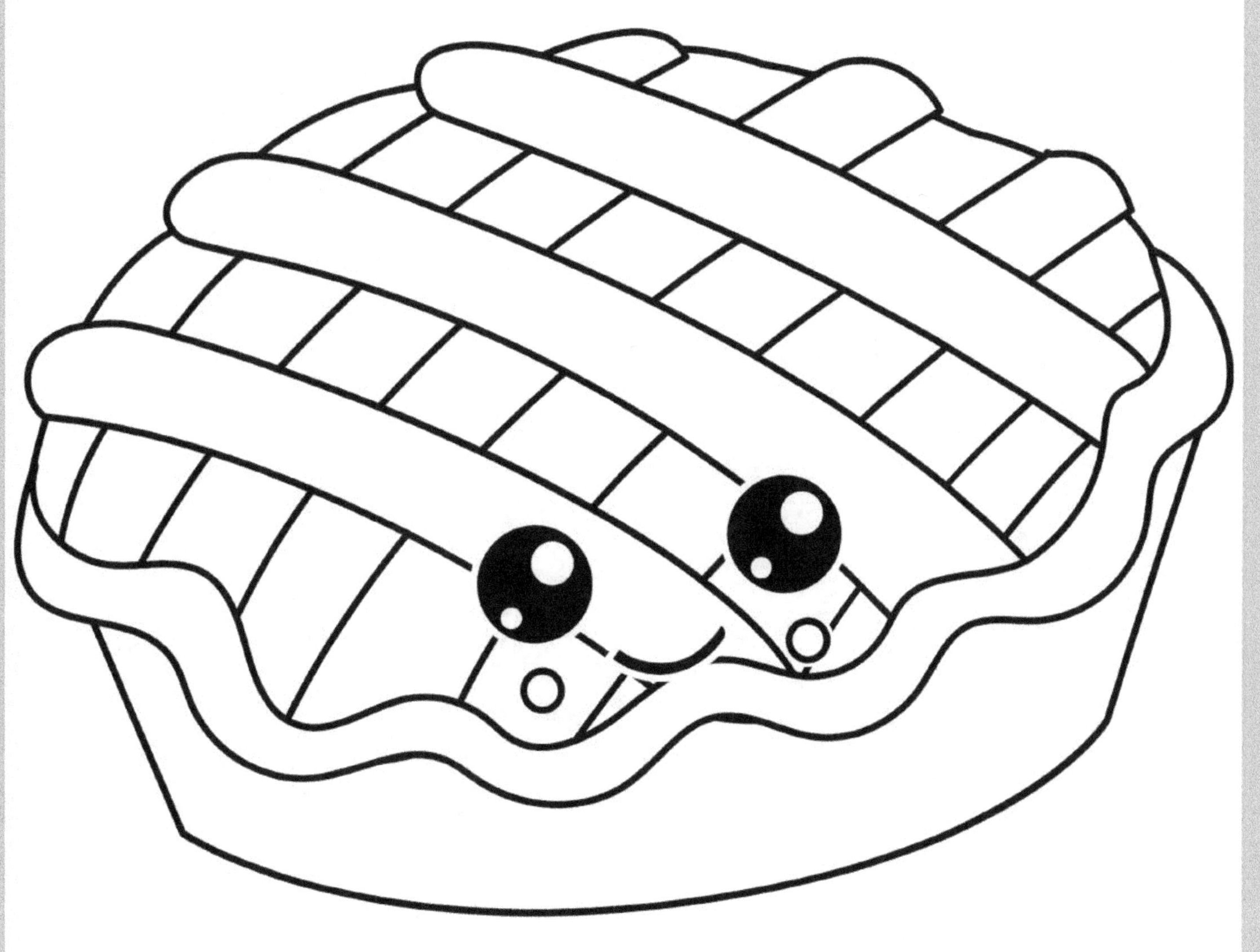

Love Muffins

THANK YOU FOR COMPLETING OUR COLORING
BOOK .
YOU CAN FIND MORE COLORING BOOK ON OUR
AMAZON SHOP (REPUTABLE DESIGN)
THANK YOU IN ADVANCE FOR LEAVING A NICE
COMMENT ON THIS COLORING BOOK .